Read-About® Holidays

Valentine's Day

By David F. Marx

Consultant
Katharine A. Kane, Reading Specialist
Former Language Arts Coordinator
San Diego County Office of Education

Children's Press®
A Division of Grolier Publishing
New York   London   Hong Kong   Sydney
Danbury, Connecticut

Visit Children's Press® on the Internet at:
http://publishing.grolier.com

Designer: Herman Adler Design Group
Photo Researcher: Caroline Anderson

Library of Congress Cataloging-in-Publication Data

Marx, David F.
    Valentine's Day / by David F. Marx.
      p. cm. — (Rookie read-about holidays)
    Includes index.
    ISBN 0-516-22212-0 (lib. bdg.)   0-516-27179-2 (pbk.)
    1. Valentine's Day—Juvenile literature. [1. Valentine's Day.
2. Holidays.] I. Title. II. Series.
GT4925.M37   2001
394.2618—dc21

                          00-022639

Can you think of someone you love?

On Valentine's Day,
we show the people
we love how much
we care about them.

Many different stories
explain how Valentine's
Day began.

One story tells of a man
named Valentine. He lived
hundreds of years ago.

8

Valentine lived in a
place where the law
did not allow people
to get married.

Valentine thought that
law was wrong. He
secretly helped many
people get married.

Valentine was put in jail
for breaking the law.

From jail, he wrote a letter
to a woman he loved.

He signed the letter,
"From your Valentine,"
because that was his name.

11

Today, we celebrate Valentine's Day on February 14 every year.

On this holiday, we send
cards called valentines
to people who are special
to us.

Many people write "I love you" or "Be my valentine" on their cards.

On Valentine's Day,
some people also give
each other flowers,
candy, or other gifts.

Children might eat candy hearts that say "I like you" or "Be mine."

19

Does Valentine's Day make you think of hearts, roses, or chocolates?

These things sometimes mean love or friendship.

They are all part of Valentine's Day.

Do you give valentine cards to your friends? You can make them yourself.

You can use pink and red paper. You can draw and cut out hearts. You can add ribbon and glitter.

Making valentines can be fun.

You can mail valentines to your friends and relatives.

People in America mail millions of valentines every year.

That is a lot of mail!

It is a wonderful feeling to open an envelope and find a valentine inside. It means someone cares about you!

29

Words You Know

candy

hearts

roses

Valentine

valentines

31

Index

About the Author

David F. Marx is an author and editor of children's books.
He resides in the Chicago area.

Photo Credits

Photographs ©: Corbis-Bettmann: 12 (Lyn Hughes), 7; Dan Brody: 15, 16;
Envision: 19, 30 left (Daryl Solomon); Folio, Inc.: 21, 31 top left (Michael
Althaus), 21 inset (John Burwell); Hulton Getty/Liaison Agency, Inc.: 11;
Nance S. Trueworthy: 26, 29; North Wind Picture Archives: 8, 31 top right;
PhotoEdit: 5 (Bill Aron), 25, 30 right (Mary Kate Denny), cover (Will Hart);
Stock Boston: 6 (Bob Daemmrich), 17 (Charles Gupton); Stone: 3 (David
Young-Wolff); The Image Works: 13, 31 bottom (Dion Ogust), 22 (Skjold).